Seeking God

Inspirational quotations to bring you closer to God

Lorna Arthur

Lorna Arthur works in a career information library where each day she meets people of all ages and religions who are seeking to build a meaningful life. She also spent six years teaching faith and values to teenagers at a Christian school in Perth. Although Lorna was born and studied in England, she now lives in the capital city of Australia, Canberra. She enjoys writing and meeting new people, and is married with two teenage sons.

Her first book, **Rocky Road**, contains stories and parables about the Christian life, and it can be ordered through Autumn House.

First published in 2006
Copyright © 2006
All rights reserved. No part of this publication
may be reproduced in any form without prior
permission from the publisher.
British Library Cataloguing in Publication Data.
A catalogue record for this book is available
from the British Library.

ISBN 1-903921-34-1

Published by Autumn House
Grantham, England.
Printed in Thailand

Seeking God

*Inspirational quotations to
bring you closer to God*

Lorna Arthur

Dedicated with much love to my husband Dale

Introduction

Do you know where God is?

Like you, I have been looking for him all my life, and we are in good company.

Since time began, people have been searching for God. They have climbed to remote caves. They have erected stone cathedrals, and when the hammers have ceased, sat in the living silence hoping to hear his voice. They have covered temples with gold. But has anyone, ever, found God?

Have you?

The brief thoughts recorded here are just like footprints in the sand, that show where I have been in my search for God. Some of the paths may seem familiar, some new, but they all have one purpose – to seek God, and to find him. Often the search for God leads us to enter a particular religion, and sometimes it leads us out of a destructive religion.

Wherever we tread, we are promised that our quest will not be in vain, because whoever we are, or wherever we have come from, God has promised us that if we look for him, we will find him, if we search for him wholeheartedly.

But that is still only half the story.

Faith is essentially about relationship, and craving reunion with a lost love. In this sense, God is searching too. He calls out from the pages of Genesis, and his voice echoes throughout the gospels, and into Revelation:

'Where are you, Adam? Where are you, Eve?

'Where are *you*?'

Though you and I cannot see God now, we are promised that one day we will see him as he is. Until then, if we listen, we can hear him calling, and one day we will see him face to face, and know him soul to soul, and be at peace.

Until then, enjoy the journey,

Blessings!

Lorna

In the beginning God

God does not come in a pocket-sized version.

Acceptance

*I promise you, if you come to me,
I will not turn you away,
not for anything. Jesus*
(See John 6:37.)

*God, in being quite comfortable
with who he is, is not threatened
in any way with who we are.*

Attention

Most of us suffer from a form of attention deficit disorder. Even as adults we act like children, calling out from the top of a wall, 'Look at me, look at me.' We try to out-do each other to gain God's attention. Yet what Christianity seeks to teach us is that, long before we set foot on a wall of works, God noticed us, sought us, and loved us.

Belief

*What I believe about God
does not change God.
It changes me.*

*Something can be true,
whether or not I believe it.
Something can be false,
whether or not I believe it.*

*Although I **believe** that God
exists I do not **know** that God
exists. I acknowledge the
limits of my own intellect.
I walk by faith and not by sight.*

*We are mortal. God is immortal.
So why do we continue to be so
surprised that God thinks and
acts so differently from us?*

Change

*The only prayer that gives God
the right to change a person is,
'God, please change me.'*

*If I try to re-make someone
in my image,
neither of us will be re-made
into the image of God.*

Children

*If you put the 'fear of God'
into children,
why are you so surprised when
they flee from you, and from God,
as an adult?*

*Long before they have heard or
understood a word we have said,
we have taught our children
about trust in God. Babies learn
trust with every warm hug,
every whisper of love, and every
sip of warm milk. In this way we
tell them that life is good, and
that they can openly trust
themselves to it.*

*If you want your children to
believe that God is love, hug them.
Even when you need to correct
their behaviour, continue to
embrace them.*

Comfort

Even if I am walking where everything is dark, and death seems to lurk around the next bend, your Word, O God, will support and comfort me. David.

(See Psalm 23:4.)

Everything will be all right. Relax now and rest. I am here, take comfort in Me. God. (See Isaiah 40:1-2.)

Life gives all of us a hard time. Often, the only punishment people need, they are already receiving as a consequence of their actions. So don't add to their troubles. Instead forgive them and comfort them, otherwise they may become so discouraged that they will be overwhelmed with despair and want to give up everything. Above all, reaffirm your love for them. Paul. (See 2 Corinthians 2:6-8.)

Compassion

True compassion is not an act of the will. It rises unbidden when we identify as an equal with the person in pain. It comes from the acknowledgement of our common humanity. God identified with us in a similar way when, as a human being, he chose to be called Immanuel. There are times in life when we simply long to be wrapped in the warm blanket of another's compassion. There are times in life when our enemy feels the same way.

Forgiveness and Understanding

Compassion and forgiveness are cousins, linked by their common relation, understanding.

He could have mocked the crowd of empty seekers. He could have called them stupid suckers. Instead he saw their weariness, their hunger and their suffering, feeling nothing but compassion. He fed them.

(See the story in Matthew 9:36.)

Creativity

Like Father, like daughter.

*Creativity is in the genes.
Inherited from the Paternal side.*

*Creating an object or character
of beauty, is in a way an
act of worship.*

*Creativity is the celebration
of God in us.*

*When a person is creative, they
revel in being unique. As fresh
energy flows through them, they
become the choreographer of their
own dance.*

Constancy

My parents forgot me once. They were so busy catching up with friends that they did not notice they had left me behind.

But I can assure you, I am more reliable. Even if your parents have sometimes ignored you, I will never forget you. God.

(See Isaiah 49:15.)

Death

Death is man's ultimate powerlessness, and God's ultimate opportunity.

Death involves travelling into an unknown country, with the simple belief that Jesus is your guide, and that he has a 100% success rate in bringing through alive all who trust in him.

Denial

I am mortal. God is immortal. A full realisation of both facts leads to peace with who I am, and who I can become.

To live the truth is to avoid both pride and false humility. It is simply to be. God describes himself this way when he calls himself the 'I AM'.

End Times

Those who rush to get right with God because it looks as if the end is near, are like those who hear of a rich uncle dying and rush to fuss around his bedside hoping for a bigger handout. Fortunately for us God is a Gentleman who is not easily offended. Thank God for that!

Future

Only God can see clearly into the future.

The less you trust the character, capability and motives of God, the more you seek to accumulate facts about the end of time. In contrast, the more you trust God, the less you need to know about the 'when' and 'how' of his Second Coming, and the more you seek to enjoy his company today

God

We but glimpse God through the bars of our humanity; though the bit we see is small, we tend to consider it all.

Immortal Being

God is an immortal Being who will take on death, so mortals can take on life.

True love

We know we love our neighbour when we do not have to borrow any sugar but we pop around for a chat anyway. We know we love God when we are right with him but continue to visit him anyway.

Not a violent father

*God is not a violent father or
an abusive husband.
God embodies love.*

*It is laughable to suggest that a
mortal human can ever be an
expert on the immortal God.*

Maximum returns

*It is in the nature of commercial business to sell the minimum of a product or service in order to get maximum returns.
In contrast it is in the nature of God to give the maximum of himself, so all will return.*

Everlasting optimist

When God was at a loss for words to express his love adequately, he came himself, in the flesh, to demonstrate his love in action.

God: the everlasting optimist!

The ultimate

God is the ultimate lateral thinker.

What kind of person is God? Well, he can change a violent, arrogant and self-opinionated man like Saul, into a man like Paul, who writes about love. So he can transform you, too, if you are willing. That's what God is like.

First

God is either first, or he does not feature. One cannot tack God onto life as an afterthought, or tuck him into a drawer like a life insurance policy.

Good

If you possess the divinely bestowed ability to enjoy the good, and make bad into good, you will never be without material to work on, and never be defeated.

Dark Friday

On that dark Friday long ago, as Jesus hung on the cross, his death seemed like the greatest calamity mankind could suffer. All hope appeared to die. Yet when Jesus reclaimed his life on that Easter morning, he turned the cross into a symbol of hope.

He can bring good out of our darkest moments.

Storm

A sudden storm of troubles can hit us hard, and leave us feeling lost. But God, who sees beyond time, can bring us through it, to the calmer water beyond.

Good News

What would you like to say to the people at church, if you had the chance? Jesus had that opportunity, and chose to read from Isaiah, chapter 61. 'I have come to bring you good news and encourage those who are in despair. I have come to heal your broken hearts, and set you free from the doubts that bind you. I want you to know that, right now, you are accepted by God.'

Your future – with God

*Your life may appear
to be disintegrating.
All you have planted may
have been uprooted.
But this is not
the picture God sees.
He sees a future for you
where beauty and joy return,
where the things you
plant will grow,
and you yourself will
flourish.*

(See Isaiah 61:3.)

Grace

*Grace both acknowledges need,
and fulfils it.*

*If, by God's grace,
I hate very little about myself,
I find little to hate in you.*

He is

*Grace is not just
something God shows,
it is something he is.*

Guilt

Guilt is not meant to be a chronic disease. It is more like a taxi, to take you from your pain and sin to the Saviour and healing.

Don't hang on

To hang on to guilt is to reject the sacrifice that Jesus made to remove your guilt.

Guilt requires confession and action, not wallowing.

The Holy Spirit

How can we love God and fear his Spirit? For the Spirit is the one who brings God's challenging, guiding, comforting and everlasting love to us.

Spirit within

*Long ago God's Spirit moved
upon the face of the waters,
and life sprang up.
Today his Spirit moves within us,
and whatever we allow him to
touch is healed and so lives.*

Hope

*You may not be able to see it yet,
but I have already planned a
future full of peace for you,
so your life can be lived
with a steady courage,
because in me you have
an eternal hope. God.*

(See Jeremiah 29:11-14.)

Tomorrow

*Hope is as much about yesterday
as about tomorrow.
If we have a history of winning,
we can convince ourselves that
we can do it again.
Likewise, when we say we
have 'hope in God'
what we are really saying
is that experience of his
involvement in our past
leads us to trust him
right now with our future.*

The Judge

Jesus was picked as the Judge because he was experienced at handling temptations and widely travelled.
For can there be any greater distance to cross, than from the culture of heaven to the culture of earth?

Humility

Humility is not about being less, but being more. It is 'I am', sitting on the lap of 'I AM'.
Content.

Like a child

Humility is pictured as grovelling before others, or before a vengeful God. In fact, it's like a child who has just received a beautiful gift, who dances with joy, hugs her father, then runs to show everyone what he has given her.

Love

We have love for one person and not another. For us, love is fickle and selective. By contrast, God has love at his core. It is not simply what he does, but who he is.

Enemies

We seek to love our enemies,
but find it impossible in the
face of their obvious faults.
So we give up.
Perhaps, instead, we should
seek to **understand** our
enemies and then,
unconsciously,
we shall begin to love them.

Pass it on

*God loves us for who we are,
so we can pass on the favour.*

Cause and effect

In our eyes, miracles involve asking God to suspend the laws of cause and effect. Yet the God who calmed stormy water is not ruled by his own rules.
He makes them.

Miracles

We often request a demonstration of God's grace in the physical world. He desires to demonstrate his grace in our spirit, for that is permanent.

His wisdom

Sometimes miracles involve asking God, in his wisdom, to reverse what we have caused with our lack of wisdom.

Patience

When Moses asked God to introduce himself, God listed 'long-suffering' as one of his skills. This is not a term we commonly use, but it highlights what is at the core of patience: the willingness to suffer ourselves, rather than spoil another's chances. This involves waiting, watching, supporting and hoping, all for another's success. Patience then, is unselfish love in action.

(See Exodus 34:5, 6.)

Peace

On earth we feel at peace when we are comfortable and safe, but circumstances can quickly change, and we lose our peace. Through the saving power of Jesus, God offers us permanent peace, regardless of our circumstances.

Rest

You cannot command rest, create rest, or buy rest. You can only enter into the rest that God has already made available in Jesus.

Soul makeover

God does not expect us to work 24/7. He told us to take a day off once a week, and book in for a soul makeover.

Holy day

'Give me a break!'

'Certainly. How would you like to take a day off this weekend and have a holy day?'

'Sounds great. Which day did you have in mind?'

Sabbath rest

Have we missed the point of the Sabbath rest? It's not just when we stop work. It has a far deeper meaning.
It highlights our ongoing need to 'stop works,' that is, to stop the struggle to achieve our own salvation, and instead accept the free gift of salvation in Jesus.

Restoration

Originally we were children of God. Through his restoring grace we still are.

Transformation

When we pray for grace, and ask for restoration, we may still feel as broken as before. In this world we receive only a taste of the total and eternal transformation God has promised.

Rebuilt

Do not lose heart. The God who could create a world from chaos, can rebuild a life from chaos too. He just needs the owner's permission.

Salvation

The whole point of finding our salvation in Christ is that we do not have to spend time looking for it any more, so we are free to spend time on others.

His job

Jesus has not called us to save the world. That's **his** job description. But he has called us to share his love with the world.

Bread of life

Once you know the Bread of Life, every other blessing is simply icing on the cake.

Saved

It was while people 'couldn't give a damn' that Jesus died to save them from damnation.

Security

Our security is not in walls, bank accounts, beauty or brains, all of which can be destroyed. It is in God, whom no one can destroy.

Self

If you are becoming a whole person you have no desire to break someone else.

Shame

No human being can rightfully say, 'Shame on you.' We can only say, 'Shame on us.' God could say 'Shame on you,' but instead he said, 'Put the shame on me, so they can go free.'

Sin

Sin is simply how a being, separated from the Source of Life, naturally behaves. Therefore it is not by an act of the will that I stop sinning, but by reconnection.

Not magic

We are taught to pray, 'Please forgive my sins,' but saying this phrase at the end of each day teaches us nothing about why we sinned, so we repeat the sin the next day. What would happen if we prayed instead, 'Dear God, please reveal to me the fear that caused me to sin,' and then we openly and honestly considered the answer?

The answer?

We are used to the fact that our simple prayers can bring forgiveness, but maybe we still need to learn that our thoughtful prayers can bring transformation.

Stay connected

How tempting it is to slip into sin
when we are suffering!
To give up on all we value when
the road ahead seems rocky!
Yet that is the time we most need
to remain connected to God – not
to continue to struggle on, as we
fear, but to rest in his arms, till
things become clear.

The cure

In health, prevention is less costly than cure. In the area of spiritual health the same principle applies. So, go to God when you are tempted, rather than wait till you have slipped and fallen.

Temptation

Temptation is quick-witted but petulant, so if you try to argue with it, it will usually win. Ignore it and give your attention to something else, and it will usually become offended and sulk away.

Be positive

Temptation is fuelled by emotion not logic, so use positive emotions to combat it.

Service done

Our temptations can do us a service, because they can show us areas in which our souls are hungry. The only trouble is, temptations only offer plastic food. Instead of falling for their menu, look for healthy ways to nourish your soul.

Thirst

I am an expert on thirst. Thirst for water, thirst for love, thirst for understanding, thirst for friendship, thirst for belonging, thirst for meaning.

*Jesus is **the** expert on thirst.*

Walking

*Christians walk **with** God, not as God.*

Worry

If you look at how few of you there are, you will become discouraged, so consider instead how happy it will make God to fling open the gates of heaven to you all, and usher you into his wide and open kingdom.

(See Luke 12:32.)

You

God invites you to be his soulmate. What do you say?

Belief

*It is our hidden, unexamined
and unchallenged beliefs that
shape us the most.
The 'shoulds' that are carved into
our soft souls in childhood.*

Choosing Belief

Information and experience form beliefs, beliefs then form attitudes and actions. All new information is filtered through the lenses of my gender, personality, age, culture and previous beliefs and, as I grow older, these glasses thicken and may become more opaque. In a very real sense, I **choose** what I believe.

Parental choice

In all families and cultures people pass on to their children tips for surviving in life. When they pass on religious ideas they are doing the same thing, with the hope that this will ensure their child's eternal life.

Change

As Christians we glibly speak of changing hearts, minds, thoughts and behaviours. To what end?

What assumptions are we making when we push for change? What are we expecting to happen?

The more I tell people how they should change, the more they tell me where to go.

Choice to change

I will do almost anything for you except change. I will change only for myself – perhaps from what I see in you.

Shame her and see her care less, praise her and see her care more.

Changing others

Oh, how we want other people to change. How we long for it, pray for it, work for it.

It would make our lives so much easier, happier and richer, or so we think.

It would also save us the bother of changing ourselves.

Church

Though the church is a vehicle to convey God's grace, it sometimes gets a flat tyre.

A troublemaker is someone who rocks the boat, then persuades everyone else there's a storm at sea.

Building church

The church is not 'them,' it is you and me. We do not attend a loving church, we build it.

The church is a hospital where even the doctors are patients.

Church and adoption

Shake hands warmly when you greet someone at church, your touch may be the only one they receive all week. The church is an adoption agency. All orphans are welcome to apply.

Church and the lonely

We often see the church as just a religious institution, but it is also a social institution. Even if it is not full of perfect people, the church provides a haven for the lonely, a family for the bereaved, a training ground for leadership, and a school where social skills can be learnt.

On your own

Just as a coal cools when removed from the fire, so it is hard for you to stay on fire for God all on your own. You will burn more brightly in good company.

Often you do not need to close the back door of your church, if you pay more attention to the people walking through it.

Heart or hierarchy

The church is a blessing when it is more 'hands, feet and heart' than hierarchy.

When a group of people band together out of fear, anything is possible, the same is true when they band together out of love.

Compassion

Compassion says, 'Been there, done that' in the nicest possible way, and often without words.

Saints with haloes

When I enter the church door, broken by the demands of the week, I do not long to see a display of saints with haloes more shiny than my own. I simply want to give and receive compassion, and thus find God.

Conversion

*We misunderstand conversion.
It is often implied that we will
no longer be human once
we are saved. If this is the case,
what will we be? Super-human?
Or simply humourless?*

*Following conversion we are just
as human as before. All that has
changed is our focus, and the
source of our love supply.*

Cynics

Cynics are simply wounded idealists, and they are not healed from cynicism by being forced to face facts. They are healed from heart sickness by hope, washed down with love.

Death

Many drift slowly and heedlessly towards death all their lives, then fight desperately for their last breath. The challenge we all have is to act appropriately: to be willing to face death when it comes, but also to be willing to really relish life while we still have it in our hands.

Support

The death of a friend or loved one is a time for the living to hold on to each other, as well as all the raw pain and joy of being alive.

The proximity of death brings into stark focus the values of life, and the meaning of the resurrection.

Denial

Denial can involve trying to appear more than I am through boasting or putting others down, or less than I am through hiding my talents. Neither reveals my true state, so neither shows me where I have grown or where I still need to grow. As I face the truth about myself I am set free. Free to change. Free to be forgiven. Free to be unique.

Doubt

When doubt replaces faith it leads to pessimism, even despair. When doubt precedes faith it leads to careful analysis, reason and common sense.

By faith

To walk by faith means moving from stability to instability with each step. To walk with God means being alongside him, regardless of your own stability or lack of it.

End times

Fortunately, the qualities needed to face the end times are the same as those needed to face today: love, courage, hope and faith.

Time ends

The end of minutes and hours is a blessing to those who long for limitless time in which to celebrate life.

Living by faith

Mortals fear death, but those who have tucked within them the promise of their own immortality welcome its arrival.

This is commonly called living by faith.

Forgiveness

Forgiveness is not so much an act of the will, but an act of understanding.

To harp on and on about reconciling differences may have the opposite effect and keep the original wounds fresh.

Fundamentalism

In a cult you lose God, your neighbour, and yourself. Fundamentalism is a skeletal religious influence. It involves the bones of rules without the warm heart of flesh.

Fanaticism

Fanaticism is like sugar-coated poison. It isolates a person in a cult in the name of truth, in order to rule by lies.

Cults

A cult is the refuge of the fearful in the cave of the timid, guarded by the egocentric.

Cults box people in, presenting an artificial security that allows them to flee from the confusion of reality.

The jailer as Saviour

If you enter a cult you give another man the key to the door of your mind, and then you throw away your own key.

Cult members look to the jailer for salvation.

Choice

In contrast to accepting salvation by grace, cult members, in effect, return God's gift of free choice and choose a live grenade instead.

Fanaticism = the sound of doubting

A fanatic is someone who shouts loudly in others' ears to drown out the sound of his own doubts.

Indoctrination at its worst is little more than the passing on of old grudges and current prejudices.

Fanaticism is passion turned to poison.

Cult thinking

Cults change
'For God so loved the world'
into
'For God so backs our side'
against all comers.

God

Long ago, people believed that the Sun rotated around the Earth. Many today, with similar ignorance, believe that God rotates around them. But God is not a satellite revolving around our whims. God is much more. He is the source of all spiritual energy, warmth and light.

Light

Is God against us, and Jesus for us? No way! Jesus is essentially the transformer, who brings God's power supply to our wattage so that we are not destroyed by it but enabled to light up.

God's picture

Our picture of God infuses all our doctrine, our view of ourselves, and our opinion of others. So, who is painting the picture of God on your soul? An amateur in dim light? Or a Master artist in the bright light of the love of Jesus?

Guilt

Guilt that lingers destroys.

Healthy guilt is more cattle prod than companion. It takes you quickly to forgiveness and freedom.

Prolonged guilt is a grudge you hold against yourself.

Sadness

Guilt and sadness are not the same thing. You can be sad about someone's pain, but you may not be responsible for causing the problem, or solving it.

The Holy Spirit

*Only the Holy Spirit does not have 'mixed motives' when he seeks to convict a person. That's why convincing sinners is in **his** job description, not ours.*

The Holy Spirit is the ultimate Corporate Change Management Consultant. His services are also offered free.

Judging

It makes all the difference in the world if we see a sinner as sad, rather than bad.

Judging another person's worth or eternal destiny is simply not in a Christian's job description, and should be a sackable offence!

Not judging

It's such a relief to realise I do not need to judge you. I was wasting so much energy and time on it. Now I am free to be your friend.

Labelling

Just when I think I have formed a clear distinction between the 'Goodies' and the 'Baddies,' a Baddy does something kind, and I have to start the labelling all over again.

The gossips

The Priest was on time for church. The Levite was tardy, but he blamed the wrecks along the road. The Good Samaritan was too late for the service, but arrived just in time for the fellowship lunch – whereupon the gossips ate him!

Law

Is the law fulfilled when I no longer notice there is a law, because obeying it has become part of my natural behaviour?

Cause and effect

God's first law is not included in the Ten Commandments. It sums them up. It states that 'as we sow we will reap'. The law of cause and effect makes a formidable enemy but a steady friend.

Rebel

Which law would I love to break? The law of cause and effect. I want to eat freely, yet stay slim. I want to please myself, but have strong relationships. I want to reduce my study time, but get better grades!

Local interpretations

Paradoxically, people can agree over the universal value of human life but shed blood over local interpretations.

They can also agree over the value of marriage, but spend their married life in civil war.

Bad rules

A good law can be buried by bad rules, and suffocate to death.

Law begins where positive natural behaviour ends.

Are there laws to make you hug someone you love? No. But there are laws to stop you hurting someone you hate.

Laws are only needed when love falls short, and laws are only truly 'fulfilled', where there is love.

Love

There is no known law against love, joy, peace, patience, gentleness, goodness, faith, meekness or temperance. So, why nag or bully your family into being Christians? Instead, simply give them a serving of the Fruit of the Spirit, and see what happens.

(See Galatians 5:22, 23.)

Listen with your heart

When you are empty, with no words to express your love, simply listen with your ears, your eyes and your heart.

Salvation

God says I'm OK, and I believe his expert opinion.

When I'm afraid I act defensively, for this is the lot of mortals. When I'm assured of immortality I no longer need to act afraid, for this is the lot of a child of God.

How did you get that idea?

Wherever did you get the idea that I came into this world to condemn you? That wasn't my purpose at all! I came to earth to save you.
Jesus.
John 3:17.